A Teen Guide to

Being Eco in Your Community

Revised Edition

Cath Senker

CAPSTONE PRESS
a capstone imprint

© 2021, 2013 Heinemann Library
an imprint of Capstone Global Library, LLC
Chicago, Illinois

All rights reserved. No part of this publication may be reproduced or transmitted in any form or by any means, electronic or mechanical, including photocopying, recording, taping, or any information storage and retrieval system, without permission in writing from the publisher.

Edited by Andrew Farrow, Adam Miller, and
 Vaarunika Dharmapala
Designed by Richard Parker
Original illustrations © Capstone Global Library
 Ltd 2013
Illustrated by HL Studios
Picture research by Tracy Cummins
Originated by Capstone Global Library Ltd

**Library of Congress Cataloging-in-Publication Data
is available on the Library of Congres website.**
ISBN 978-1-4846-5841-3 (paperback revised)

Acknowledgments
Alamy: Anthony Pleva, 20, Avalon/Construction Photography, 11 top, David J. Green - electrical, 9, Peter Titmuss , 25, Rosa Irene Betancourt, 22, 23; Capstone Studio: Karon Dubke, 43, 45, 47; Getty Images: AFP/ AARON MAASHO, 13, Andrew Holt, 31, Fuse, 34, Jose Luis Pelaez Inc, 15, Jupiterimages, 41, Mark D Callanan, 6, Mikael Vaisanen, cover, Peter M. Fishe, 12; iStockphoto: SolStock, 5; LA Photo Party: Brian Miller, 33; Lothrop Science, Spanish, Technology Magnet Omaha Public Schools: Pamela Galus, 36; Newscom: REUTERS, 21; Science Source: Ted Kinsman, 10; Shutterstock: Andre Blais, 35, AVAVA, 32, Claus Mikosch, 48, Dmitriy Shironosov, 4, gillmar, 29 right, Inc, 49, jabiru, 38, Kuramyndra, 8, Leftleg, 39, manfredxy, 11 bottom, monticello, 40, Nikola Spasenoski, 14, Olivier Le Moal, design element, rangizzz, 30, Zoran Vukmanov Simokov, 29 left; SuperStock: imageBROKER, 7, Peter Bennett/ Ambient Images, 26, 37

Every effort has been made to contact copyright holders of material reproduced in this book. Any omissions will be rectified in subsequent printings if notice is given to the publisher.

All the Internet addresses (URLs) given in this book were valid at the time of going to press. However, due to the dynamic nature of the Internet, some addresses may have changed, or sites may have changed or ceased to exist since publication. While the author and publisher regret any inconvenience this may cause readers, no responsibility for any such changes can be accepted by either the author or the publisher.

Printed in the United States of America.
3492

Contents

Some words are shown in bold, **like this**. You can find out what they mean by looking in the glossary.

Important!
Please check with an adult before doing the projects in this book.

How Can I Be Eco?

We all know that human activities have a huge impact on our environment, from using up the world's resources to affecting **climate change**. We realize it makes sense to reduce that impact as much as we can. Although the problems may seem enormous, every one of us can make a difference. It is easy to get started—there are many quick, simple, and cheap things we can all do.

This book considers how you can be "eco"—or environmentally friendly—in your community. So, who *are* the members of your community? They are the people around you—your neighbors and people in stores, places of worship, and schools. Sports teams, outdoor activity clubs, and music groups are also communities.

We benefit from being part of communities, just as we thrive from having friends and family around us. If any of the communities you belong to are not involved in actions that help the environment, they might be interested in adopting some eco-friendly ideas. In addition to helping the environment, it may save them some money!

The girls at this dance club could consider making the lighting more eco-friendly.

The Bicycle Kitchen

The Bicycle Kitchen is a voluntary organization in Los Angeles, California, that helps people fix their bikes. The volunteers believe that many more people would cycle if they knew how to take care of their bikes. Cyclists can bring their broken bike and a volunteer will help them fix it, for a small donation. The group also runs workshops about repairs. Small projects like this can help to reduce car use and make neighborhoods more pleasant.

The range of issues to tackle may seem overwhelming—from saving energy and water, reducing waste, and choosing environmentally friendly food to encouraging nature and **biodiversity**. So, why not consider where you could most easily make changes, and start from there? This book has realistic projects you can do right now, with a little help from others in your community. Millions of people all over the world are doing these things. So, what are you waiting for?

The sky's the limit: Wind turbines

Local environmental groups may be able to build up to ambitious projects. Wausau East High School in Wausau, Wisconsin, has installed its own **wind turbine** to produce energy. The wind turbine provides about 5 percent of the school's power needs, saving about $14,000 a year on electricity bills.

Students use a model of a wind turbine to learn how wind power works.

What's in it for me?

By promoting and protecting nature, you can make the places where you live, study, and socialize more pleasant. You could help your family save money by reducing energy bills. If you can help reduce costs significantly, your parent or caregiver might reward you!

Why be eco-friendly at school?

Your school is an established community, so it is an easy place to start being eco-friendly. It can be good for your education, too. Working in the fresh air on outdoor gardening and nature projects makes a welcome change from sitting in a classroom. Seeing the results of your work provides great motivation to continue. Imagine spotting the first winged visitors to your nature area or harvesting your home-grown vegetables!

People all around the world enjoy nature. Here, residents of Jalisco, Mexico, are celebrating the arrival of spring.

New friends, new skills

If you become more involved in your school and local community, you will make friends with people of different ages and backgrounds while also gaining useful skills. The ability to cooperate with a variety of people and to organize activities will look good on your application when you apply to colleges or for jobs.

This vegetable patch grows in an urban garden in Detroit, Michigan. You don't have to live in the country to go green!

"By taking the concept of **sustainable** living beyond the narrow, individualistic [focused on individuals] approach, we can learn to see our interconnectedness to our environment and its inhabitants. By getting involved in our communities, by talking to our neighbors, by supporting local groups, and by re-imagining where we live, we can green not only our own lifestyles, but our streets, neighborhoods, towns, cities and, ultimately, our societies. Who knows, we may even make friends doing it."

Sami Grover, writer and environmental activist, North Carolina

Eco jobs

If you enjoy helping your local environment, you may decide to pursue a career in environmental work. Here are a few possible occupations:

- Environmental **conservation** involves managing parks and wildlife areas, waste management, and the protection of wild animals.
- Forestry includes the management of trees, forests, and woodlands.
- Within businesses, environmental officers are responsible for improving **energy efficiency** and waste management.
- **Nongovernmental organizations** need people to undertake practical conservation, educate the public, and raise awareness about specific issues.
- Newspapers and television programs need writers and researchers who are knowledgeable about the environment.

YOUR COMMUNITY:
Energy, Water, and Waste

Reducing energy and water use and reducing the waste we produce may sound like huge tasks, but there are several simple actions you can easily adopt at home, at school, at a community center, and at other places. They will soon become habits. When many individuals work together, you can make a real difference.

Save energy, save money

Take the challenge and adopt these simple ideas for saving energy:

- When it is cold outside, do you really need to keep your home as hot as a sauna so you can go around in a T-shirt? Embrace cold weather by wearing a warm, cozy sweater.
- You tend to feel cold when you are sitting still. Instead of turning up the heat when you are watching TV or using the computer, consider snuggling up with a soft blanket around you.
- Don't stand by! It is easy to switch off appliances when you stop using them, so that you don't leave them guzzling energy in standby mode. See if you can borrow an energy monitor (see the box on page 9) to check how much energy your household is using. Then see if you could reduce it.

Snuggling up in a blanket to read can be a real pleasure.

Energy monitors

Energy monitors allow you to check how much electricity your appliances are using. The simplest ones can be connected to an appliance. There are also small wireless monitors with a transmitter (device that sends electronic signals) to connect around the cable of your electricity meter. Some energy monitors can store data, which you upload to a computer. All provide useful information about the costs of running your appliances. Try checking how much energy you are currently using at bedtime. In fact, almost every appliance except the refrigerator can be turned off!

Keep cool, avoid waste

When it is hot outside, it is tempting to crank up the air conditioning or switch on fans to keep cool. But there are ways to reduce the heat without using up large amounts of energy. For example, did you know that direct sunlight on a window can produce as much heat as a radiator? To cut out heat, close the blinds and curtains during the hottest part of the day. Open the windows in the cool of the morning and in the evening to lower the temperature. Electrical appliances and lights produce heat as well as light, so it makes sense to turn them off when not in use.

Eco impact

This diagram shows approximately how long it takes for each of these appliances to use up 1 **kilowatt hour** of energy:

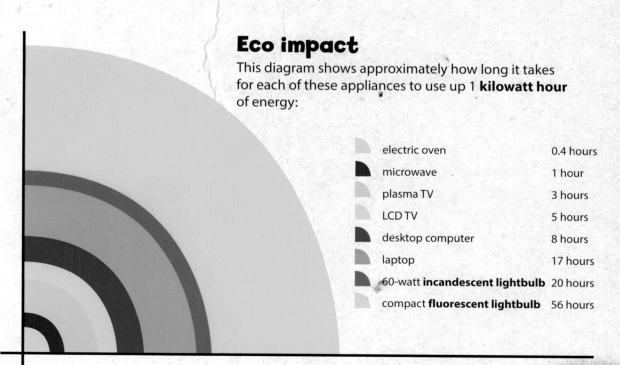

electric oven	0.4 hours
microwave	1 hour
plasma TV	3 hours
LCD TV	5 hours
desktop computer	8 hours
laptop	17 hours
60-watt **incandescent lightbulb**	20 hours
compact **fluorescent lightbulb**	56 hours

Environmental groups can help!

If you are part of a group of like-minded people, they will support you to change your habits and stick to greener ways. For help finding a group, try visiting www.nrdc.org/reference/kids.asp.

Eco Scouts

The Boy Scouts of America are going eco. In 2011, they introduced eco-friendly jerseys. The jerseys are made from Repreve, a recyclable wool produced using water bottles made of PET (a type of plastic). Normal sportswear is made from synthetic fabrics that use crude oil. Every pound (450 grams) of Repreve used saves 0.5 gallons (1.9 liters) of oil.

Some environmental groups use technology to help people save energy. For example, in the United Kingdom, the Three Villages Eco Group carries out **thermal imaging** to show people where heat is escaping from their homes. To minimize heat loss from the doors and windows, residents can put in **draft proofing** and line their curtains.

In this thermogram of a home in winter, the red areas show where heat is escaping.

Be clean and green

The way we wash has a major impact on our water usage. Don't worry—you can be squeaky clean and eco-friendly, too! If you usually take a bath, how about taking a refreshing five-minute shower instead?

Keep in mind that some powerful showers use even more water than the average bath, and that taking a long shower may have the same effect as taking a bath!

To ensure you can have a great shower while still using water responsibly, talk to your family about buying a water-saving showerhead. This small device reduces the flow of water, but you can still enjoy a powerful shower. It is quite cheap to buy and soon saves money on your utility bills. It will also reduce the amount of water that has to be extracted from rivers and the ground.

You can fit a water **flow restrictor** (shown left) to every faucet in your house to reduce the amount of water you use.

Save water

- Check that the dishwasher or washing machine is full before you run it. Are you using the most efficient energy and water settings that you can use?
- Try using a sink full of water to wash a large pile of dishes twice a day rather than washing every time you have a snack or drink.
- While you are waiting for the water to run hot when you are doing the dishes, you could fill up a bowl with cooler water for rinsing.
- When you are washing your hands or face, plug the drain and run only the water you need.
- You could use leftover glasses of water to pour over your plants, rather than wasting this water.

How to tackle waste

It is not hard to reduce, reuse, and recycle and still have everything you need! Some people like to add a fourth "R"—refuse to purchase. Before you buy something, think carefully about whether or not you really need it. For example, you might want access to a product, but you do not really need to own it. You can read the latest magazines and newspapers in a library for free. It is also free to borrow library books and cheap to rent DVDs. For the purchases you do need, invest in a durable shopping bag so you can avoid using plastic bags.

When you shop, try to find items made from recycled material.

Swap or sell

Reusing goods is simple, too. See if you can join a Freecycle group in your area. People give away goods they no longer need rather than throwing them away. (Check with a parent before you join and always go with a trusted adult to collect items.) Or why not hold a garage sale and sell those old toys, games, and clothes? You will learn some bargaining skills and hopefully make some money.

Buying secondhand products is another great idea. How about investing in some vintage clothing? An interesting, original item from a thrift store will help you stand out from the crowd.

Recycling

You probably already recycle paper, cardboard, and plastic. Did you know that you can also recycle household items such as batteries, CDs, DVDs, and lightbulbs? Check your local government web site to find out where to take them. Of course, recycling is not effective unless people buy the new goods produced, so look out for interesting products made from recycled materials.

Eco impact

Vehicle tires are designed to be extremely tough and resistant to chemicals, and they do not melt. They are made from nylon fabrics and metal covered with hard rubber. Once they have worn down, car users have to replace them. In the United States, about 300 million tires are thrown away each year. One company, Liberty Tire Recycling, collects and recycles about one-third of the country's scrap tires to make rubber goods, landscaping materials, adhesives, or fuel.

This woman runs a successful business in Ethiopia, making shoes from recycled tires and fabrics.

Being green: Summing up

- Save energy by wearing warm clothing at home when it is cold outside.
- Turn off appliances when not in use.
- Take quick showers to stay clean and fresh.
- Use only the water you need.
- Keep reducing, reusing, and recycling.

Nature and Biodiversity

How can you make your neighborhood nature-friendly? Perhaps there is a nature club in your area that you could join. Otherwise, why not gather some friends and neighbors together to encourage wildlife in your local area?

You can plant herbs and wildflowers to attract beneficial (helpful) insects such as butterflies, bees, and ladybugs. Bees and butterflies **pollinate** plants, while ladybugs feed on aphids (small insects that damage plants). Make sure the varieties you choose are suitable for your local climate. These are all quite easy to grow:

Herbs: Basil, dill, fennel, lavender, parsley, thyme, sage

Flowers: Cornflower, clematis, hydrangea, zinnia

Eco impact

One-third of the human diet can be traced to bee pollination. Bees pollinate crops, so they can be fertilized and reproduce. Bee populations have dwindled, but it is easy to create a bee-friendly environment. Some organizations have asked schools and community groups to plant wildflowers and **nectar-rich** plants in the spring to help the bee populations to recover.

As these bees fly among the buttercups and daisies, they will pollinate both types of flower. Encouraging bees does not mean you will get stung, as long as you are careful.

These volunteers are planting a tree. Once it is in the soil, they will add **mulch** and water it.

Attracting the right visitors

There is nothing worse than planting herbs and flowers only to find they have been munched on by insects. Luckily, there are several ways to encourage beneficial insects and to deter harmful ones naturally, without harming wildlife or the environment. A popular method is companion planting, which means combining plants that help each other by deterring pests. For example, plant chives or garlic to repel aphids. Dill attracts beneficial insects such as hoverflies and wasps that eat aphids. Find out more at http://kgi.org/companion-planting-chart.

The benefits of trees

Trees play an important role in our environment. In places that are prone to flooding, they retain water and reduce the run-off of water. Coastal Louisiana was badly affected by Hurricane Katrina in 2005. Several students from local schools in St. Bernard Parish—Chalmette High School and St. Bernard Middle School—lost their homes in the disaster. As Ashley, 18, says, "After Katrina, we lived in Houston for nine months. We had to tear down our home and start a new one." In 2011, students from these schools took part in planting 300 cypress trees by the Mississippi River. This will help to protect the land from future flooding.

Attracting birds

You could make a small birdhouse, also called a nesting box, with a hole to attract many different local species of birds. It is wise to find out about the kinds of birds that nest locally, so that you make the right kind of home for them. For information, try www.birds.cornell.edu/Page.aspx?pid=1139.

Why make a nesting box?

Many bird species depend on holes in trees and buildings to make their nest. These sites disappear when woods and gardens are developed and people repair old houses. Nesting boxes can help make up for the loss.

Putting up your nesting box

Attach your box at the end of winter, using galvanized (rust-proof) or stainless-steel nails. Check it will be sheltered from the **prevailing wind**, rain, and strong sunlight. The front of the nest should be angled slightly downward, to prevent rain from dripping into it. Put the box 3 to 10 feet (1 to 3 meters) above the ground on a tree, a wall, or the side of a shed. Check predators such as squirrels cannot reach the nest. Also check it is not near bird feeders, so visiting birds won't disturb the nesting birds. For more information, see www.nwf.org/Get-Outside/Outdoor-Activities/Garden-for-Wildlife/Gardening-Tips/Attracting-Nesting-Birds.aspx.

Make a nesting box for birds

You will need:

A plank of wood 6 x 46 inches (15 x 117 cm) and at least 0.6 inches (1.5 cm) thick. (It makes sense to allow a little extra, in case something goes wrong.)
A saw
A drill
A pencil
Galvanized or stainless-steel nails
Waterproof material such as car tire inner tube to make the hinge

Please ask an adult to supervise this project.

Method:

1. Saw the parts to the sizes shown in the diagram.

2. Drill small holes in the base piece to drain out rainwater.

3. Drill a hole in the front piece. It should be the correct size for the bird you have in mind. For example, it should be about 1½ inches (3.8 cm) to attract bluebirds.

4. Drill a hole in the back piece to attach the nesting box.

5. Mark in pencil where the sides, roof, and base will fit on to the back piece.

6. Cut a groove in the back piece where the roof will slot in. Make sure the roof fits snugly.

7. Nail the sides to the back piece, then nail on the base.

8. Nail the front to the sides and base.

9. Make a hinge to attach the roof. First, cut the rubber to the width of the box. Then, nail the rubber along the back of the box and to the roof. Finally, attach the box to a tree.

Source: National Nest Box Week, www.bto.org/nnbw/index.htm

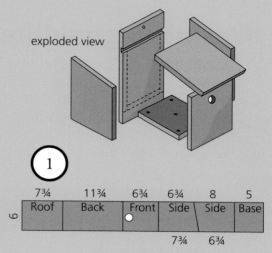

exploded view

①

7¾	11¾	6¾	6¾	8	5
Roof	Back	Front	Side	Side	Base

7¾   6¾

plank size 6 x 46 in.

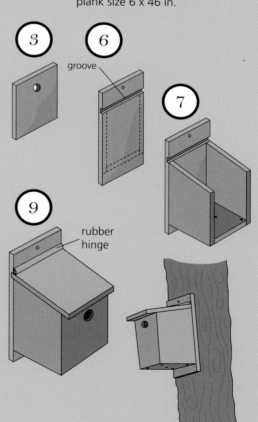

③   ⑥

groove

⑦

⑨

rubber hinge

Attracting wildlife

A small pond is a wonderful way to attract wildlife. Before you start, there are some points to consider. Can you position your pond away from overhanging trees and in partial shade? You will need to think about the shape of your pond. It should have shallow areas to allow creatures to get in and out easily and to allow birds to bathe. It is important to get the right balance of plants, too.

Build a small pond

You will need:

A shovel

Pond liner, bought from a garden center or online (try to buy one that is recycled or made from rubber). Use this formula to figure out how much you need: (length + [depth x 2]) + (width + [depth x 2]). For example, if your pond is 8 ft. (2.5 m) long by 5 ft. (1.5 m) wide, and 3 ft. (1 m) deep, you'll need: 8 + 6 + 5 + 6 ft. = 25 ft. (2.5 + 2 + 1.5 + 2 m = 8 m) of pond liner.

Soft sand

A few rocks

Long grass seed (optional)

Plants

Please ask an adult to supervise this project.

Method:

1. Measure the area of the pond.

2. Dig the hole. Start with a hole at least 2 ft., 7 in. (80 cm) deep at one end. The other end should come up at a slope of 20°.

3. Remove sharp stones or roots. Leave a step on which to later place shallow water plants.

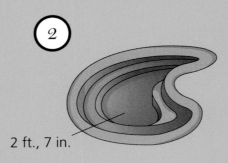

2

2 ft., 7 in.

Aquatic plants

To keep your pond healthy, try planting these:

• Oxygenators are important for keeping the water clear. Try elodea or American Vals.

• Floating plants provide shelter for animals. You could try water shield or mosquito fern.

• Marginal plants grow around the edge of the pond, providing protection from predators for creatures like frogs. Arrowhead is an example.

• Deep-water aquatics are planted deep. Their leaves help keep the pond cool and provide shelter. You could plant cabomba or hornwort.

Being green: Summing up

- Plant herbs and wildflowers to encourage beneficial insects.
- Plant trees to help improve the environment.
- Make a nesting box to give shelter to birds.
- Build a pond to attract wildlife.

4. Add a layer of sand to the pond.

5. Place the pond liner in the hole, allowing for an overlap of 12 to 20 in. (30 to 50 cm).

6. Place a few rocks around the shallow end. Mammals will be able to lean off them to drink the water.

7. If you would like to attract frogs, plant some long grass seed around the deep end to provide shelter from predators and shade from the Sun.

8. If possible, fill the pond with rainwater. Otherwise, use tap water, but leave it for two weeks before adding plants, to allow any chemicals to evaporate.

9. Add some aquatic (water-living) plants.

10. Cover the edge of the liner to protect it—for example, with turf or slate.

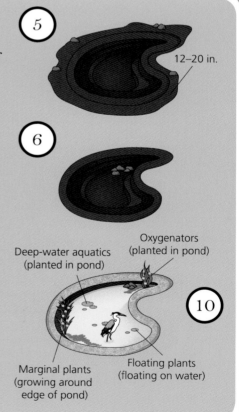

5

12–20 in.

6

Oxygenators (planted in pond)

Deep-water aquatics (planted in pond)

10

Marginal plants (growing around edge of pond)

Floating plants (floating on water)

A Healthy Neighborhood

Is your town or city a mess? It's not hard to improve it a little. Simple tasks such as making posters to persuade people to use garbage cans or to clean up dog waste can help your neighbors to clean up their act. It is also worth reminding people that it is illegal to drop litter, and that they can be fined for doing so. You could even get together with friends to organize a litter pickup (see page 23), plant some herbs, or encourage more walking and cycling.

Does this sound unrealistic? Well, it has been shown that people make the choice whether to litter, so putting up signs to focus attention on the issue can make a real difference. Keep Australia Beautiful ran a competition to create a 30-second advertisement with an anti-littering message aimed at people under 25. Robbie Reid was one of the young people who took up the challenge. He produced an anti-litter ad with a cute animated crab named Kevin, who advised viewers to "stash trash" in the garbage can. Robbie won an award of $1,000!

Much of this trash could have been recycled. You can see paper, cardboard, a can, and plastic bottles. The plastic bags could have been reused.

Littering: The facts

Keep America Beautiful carried out a survey of littering and discovered that:

- Nearly one in five people (17 percent) dropped litter in a public place, while most (83 percent) disposed of it properly.
- People are more likely to litter if the area is already littered. In contrast, if there are recycling and garbage cans handy, people tend to use them.
- Littering is an individual choice. People who believe littering is wrong use garbage cans. Individuals can encourage others not to litter and help to change habits.

An herb patch

Once you've tackled the garbage ... how about community food growing? Is there a patch of unused ground in your area? If you are part of a community eco group, you could seek permission from your local government to plant some herbs for everyone to use. Or perhaps a local community center has a space where you could grow plants in pots. It is easy to do, and your cooking will be tastier with fresh herbs.

Rooftop gardens

Tokyo, Japan, is a densely populated city. Few people have gardens. In recent years, however, people have developed an interest in growing their own food. Since space is an issue, these gardeners are ingenious, creating vegetable plots in front of railroad stations and making rooftop gardens. Businesses have become involved, too. For example, in 2011, East Japan Railway opened a rental garden on the rooftop of the Lumine Ogikubo Building. People can rent plots to grow fruits and vegetables in addition to using the garden to relax and socialize.

Litter

Is there an area near you that is ruined by litter? Why not organize a litter pickup? You could start with a small cleanup—for example, on your school's fields. Perhaps you could ask students, parents, and teachers to sponsor you to raise the money you'll need for equipment.

These volunteers in Little Haiti (above) and Baynanza Biscayne Bay (page 23), both in Miami, Florida, are taking part in a community day to clean up their neighborhoods.

Stay safe!

It is important to find an adult to supervise your event, in case you find dangerous materials. Make sure everyone in your group knows that if they spot syringes, they should not touch them. Syringes can cause injury or infection. After the litter pickup, contact members of your local government and tell them where you found the materials.

Organize a community litter pickup

Here's how to plan your litter pickup:

1. Find some friends to form an organizing group and an adult to support you.

2. You may need to get permission to work in your chosen area. Ask an adult to help you to check about **public liability insurance**.

3. Pick a day and time for the event. Two hours should be enough.

4. Publicize the event. You could tell the local media.

5. With an adult, carry out a **risk assessment** of the area. There may be hazards, such as broken glass or syringes.

6. Find equipment. You can ask everyone to bring strong gloves and garbage bags. You'll also need litter pickers and reflective vests, if possible. It is helpful to have some bags and containers to store sharp objects and tape to seal them. Make sure you have a first aid kit. If your group joins Keep America Beautiful, you may receive a grant (money to help).

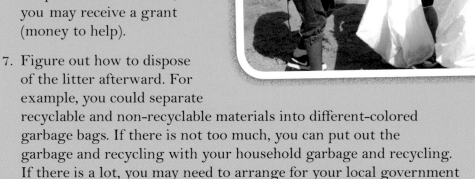

7. Figure out how to dispose of the litter afterward. For example, you could separate recyclable and non-recyclable materials into different-colored garbage bags. If there is not too much, you can put out the garbage and recycling with your household garbage and recycling. If there is a lot, you may need to arrange for your local government to pick it up or take it to your local waste and recycling center.

8. Celebrate your work! It is worth taking "before" and "after" photos and sending them to the media. If you have done well, you are bound to get plenty of support for your next litter pickup.

Source: LitterAction, www.litteraction.org.uk

Get on your bike!

We all know that vehicles use up precious **fossil fuels** and create air pollution. But how easy is it to change how you travel? Maybe you could start with a small change in your habits, such as replacing one journey a week in a vehicle by cycling or walking.

Cycling and walking

Cycling has many good points, such as these:
- Cycling and walking are good for your health.
- Cycling is cheap, and walking costs nothing.
- The more people walk or cycle, the less traffic there is on the roads.
- Many towns and cities have bike lanes, often making it faster to use a bike than a car.
- On a bike, you can zip through traffic and park in many places.
- If you enjoy nature, you are more likely to see interesting plants and animals than you would in a car.
- Cycling is a popular sport that allows you to meet new people.
- Your bike needs regular maintenance to keep it in good working order, but it is quite simple once you know how.

Cycling also has some bad points, including these:
- Cycling or walking may not be practical for long distances.
- Road traffic can make it dangerous to cycle.
- Traffic fumes can make it unpleasant to walk or cycle.
- Many people feel unsafe walking or cycling in the dark.
- Not every climate is suitable for year-round cycling or walking. For safety, cyclists need to invest in good wet-weather gear and high-visibility clothing such as a vest with reflective stripes.

Eco impact

In the United States in 2008, just 0.5 percent of journeys to work were made by bike, while under 3 percent were made on foot. However, there was an increase in cycling to work of 43 percent between 2000 and 2008. This shows that habits can change over time.

Cycle safety

So, how can cycling be encouraged? Some simple changes can make a difference. It is helpful to have bike racks or other safe storage areas for bicycles in schools, parks, and other places in the community. Spreading knowledge about bike maintenance and safety is useful, too.

If you get involved in promoting cycling or any other eco project in your community, see if you can hold an event to promote your work and get more people involved.

Transportation survey

Ask your friends about the transportation they use, how often they use it, and the distances they travel. Figure out the average distance people walk or cycle, and how often. Ask what it would take to persuade them to walk or cycle more and farther. Which key factors would help? Repeat the survey to see if you are having an impact on the behavior of your friends.

Being green: Summing up

- Organize a litter pickup to clean up your local area.
- Put up posters to deter littering.
- Create a community garden.
- Replace some journeys with cycling or walking.

Cycling is an easy, gentle form of exercise. It helps to improve your fitness, which can reduce your risk of health problems in later life.

YOUR SCHOOL: Saving Energy and Water

Why would you want to be eco-friendly at school? First, you spend a lot of time there, so you will benefit if the school environment improves. Second, a school is a large community, so eco-friendly measures can make a real difference. Third, eco projects allow you to become more involved in the running of your school.

Eco-Schools

Has your school joined the worldwide Eco-Schools Network? It enables you to share ideas and ask for advice. For example, Slovakian schoolchildren visited schools in Berlin and Hamburg, Germany, in 2009 and learned methods for taking responsibility for eco projects.

The "Green Teens" are students from Lakeridge High School and Lake Oswego High School, from Lake Oswego, Oregon. They held a special workshop for parents and school employees to discuss tips and tools for boosting the enthusiasm of eco groups.

This community group is being given a demonstration about how to properly plant a tree.

Start small

Don't worry if your school is not in the Eco-Schools Network. To kick off some activity, how about finding out if your friends might like to become involved? Then, see if you can find at least one teacher to support your eco projects. You could set up an environmental club or become an eco class. Maybe you can get your school custodian on board or the parents, through the Parent–Teacher Association.

It might be easiest to start by focusing on one theme. For example, at Eco-School Elie Faure de Lormont, France, the students focused on waste in the first year, food in the second year, and then biodiversity in the third year.

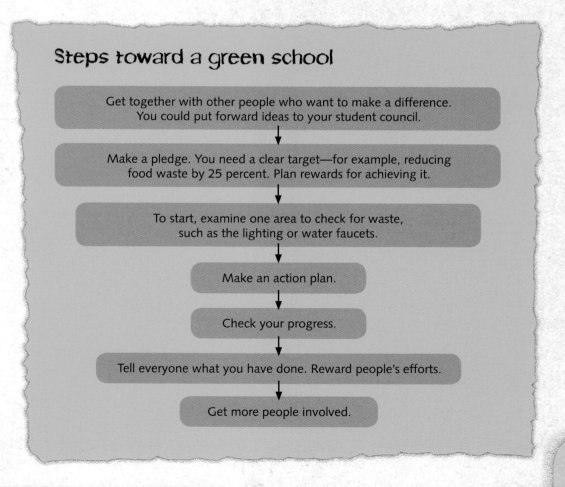

Steps toward a green school

Get together with other people who want to make a difference. You could put forward ideas to your student council.

↓

Make a pledge. You need a clear target—for example, reducing food waste by 25 percent. Plan rewards for achieving it.

↓

To start, examine one area to check for waste, such as the lighting or water faucets.

↓

Make an action plan.

↓

Check your progress.

↓

Tell everyone what you have done. Reward people's efforts.

↓

Get more people involved.

Easy energy saving

Saving energy is a great idea. But how do you know where you need to cut back? It is worth carrying out an energy review to see how much energy you are using at the moment. This document includes a model you can use: www.countdownyourcarbon.org/SchoolEnergyAudit.pdf.

The simplest way to cut energy use in schools is to look at lighting. First, you could do a survey of lights left on in empty rooms. Also look at lighting levels. You need different levels of lighting for different tasks—for example, hallways require far less light than classrooms or science labs. Some areas may have too much or too little light. You could carry out a similar survey for radiators. Are they being left on in unused rooms? Are some areas too hot or too cold?

Energy action plan

Next, work on your action plan. Start with easy actions, such as putting up signs reminding people to turn off lights when they are not needed. Studies have shown that natural light in classrooms is good for your health and helps you to learn better. So, if it is a bright day, you can switch off the lights. Another simple step is to replace the lightbulbs with energy-efficient ones. Talk with the school maintenance staff about this. You could also check whether or not the lights and heating are turned off on weekends and during school holidays.

Energy-efficient lightbulbs

Cheap, energy-efficient lightbulbs may seem like a bargain. However, they may not be as efficient as the top brands and won't save you money in the long run. Here's where a bit of math comes in handy. You can buy a lightbulb for $5.60 that has a rated life of 850 hours. The alternative is a bulb that produces the same light for 18,000 hours, but costs $62. Energy use is the same for each bulb. Which bulb is a better buy? Check your answer on page 55.

Remember to be patient with the people you are trying to persuade. Explain the benefits of your proposals clearly and allow people time to make a decision. Here's an example you could mention: Sleepy Hollow Middle School in Sleepy Hollow, New York, came up with a cheap, simple way to cut energy. Members of this community connected all their computers to a power strip. This made it effortless to switch them all off at the main power supply at the end of the day.

How long do different light sources last?

light source	efficiency (lumens/watt)	average life (hours)
standard incandescent	5–20	750–1,000
tungsten-halogen	15–25	2,000–4,000
compact fluorescent (5–26 watts)	20–55	10,000
compact fluorescent (27–40 watts)	50–80	15,000–20,000

Compact fluorescent bulbs can replace traditional incandescent bulbs in many light fixtures. Halogen lamps are a type of incandescent lighting, but they are more efficient. They are commonly used in floor and desk lamps and for flood lighting.

compact fluorescent

standard incandescent

Progress check

Once you have some energy-saving measures in place, it makes sense to carry out regular reviews to check to see if usage is being reduced. This involves doing the surveys again. Hopefully, energy use will have decreased. If not, don't despair! Perhaps the message is not getting across. Why not try to get more publicity for your campaign? If you have managed to reduce usage, celebrate your achievements—and then move on to your next campaign!

Ways to cut water waste

Another important area to tackle is water waste. You can adopt the same approach suggested for energy usage: carry out a review, develop an action plan, do a follow-up review to check progress, and assess if further action is required. Here's a sample water review that you can use: www.eeweek.org/water_wise/water_audit.

Water review

Areas to cover:
- School buildings: Find out about water use in all the buildings and calculate the amount of water used per person per day.
- Water-using devices: Discover how much water is used—for example, in the toilets, sinks, water fountains, showers, and science labs.
- School grounds: How much water is used to water the fields or gardens?

Materials you will need:
- figures for how much water the school used over the past 12 months or, if possible, the school's water bill
- a stopwatch for calculating the **flow rate** of faucets, showers, and water fountains
- **flow meter bags** or a bucket
- a camera for recording observations and presenting results.

Checking water flow

Reducing water flow from faucets can save water and cut the cost of heating water. The flow rate does not need to be more than about 2.5 gallons (9 liters) per minute. If it is more, you can fix flow restrictors (see page 11) to the faucets, so the water does not come out so fast. To check flow rate:

1. Run water into a flow meter bag or bucket for 15 seconds.
2. Measure the water. Multiply by four to get the flow rate per minute.
3. If it is more than 2.5 gallons per minute, recommend that your school buy flow restrictors.

This Ethiopian girl is transporting water in a heavy container. Many people around the world do not have the luxury of just turning on a faucet in their home or school.

Water action!

Once you have carried out a review, brainstorm ideas for an action plan. Many actions cost nothing, or very little. You could make posters to encourage people not to waste water while washing their hands. At SOS Children's Village in Imzouren, Morocco, the children performed a play to inform others about the importance of saving water. You could ask the cafeteria staff to avoid using trays when possible, to reduce the amount of dish washing. You will probably need to talk to the custodians and maintenance workers, too. Perhaps there are leaking faucets to mend, or they could cut down on using pressure washers to clean public areas.

Being green: Summing up

- Become an Eco-School or start an eco club.
- Review water and energy use.
- Develop an action plan to cut usage.
- Check progress and carry out follow-up actions as needed.
- Celebrate what you have achieved!

Cutting Waste: Simple Tips

What are the three Rs in school? Reduce, reuse, and recycle! Most school waste is paper, packaging, and food waste. There are simple ways to reduce these kinds of waste and lighten the garbage bags.

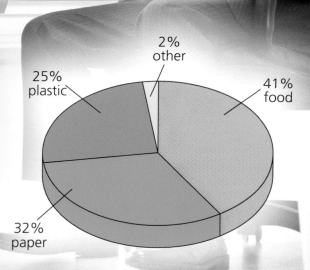

2%
other

25%
plastic

41%
food

32%
paper

At Black Mountain School in Scottsdale, Arizona, students checked the principal's waste for one day (see pie chart). They then produced a plan to help her recycle more paper and plastic.

Reduce waste

If you have to print out work at school, print double-sided so that you use half as much paper. What about litter? One Scottish student from an eco group was finding it hard to persuade others to reduce, reuse, and recycle litter. She asked for advice on the Eco-Schools forum. Another student replied that at his school, students receive praise and rewards, such as a special postcard, if they follow the litter policy.

Another worthwhile project is to reduce the use of materials you don't need at all. At Nichols School, in Buffalo, New York, the students began a movement called Plasti-Gone. They aim to persuade schools and businesses not to use single-use plastic products. For example, their "stop sucking" campaign encourages people to stop using drinking straws, which waste resources.

Paige Dedrick, Donata Lorenzo, and Caroline Fenn (from left to right) are the girls who started the Plasti-Gone movement.

Wipe Out Waste

Around Australia, schools are taking part in the Wipe Out Waste program. At Unley School, in South Australia, student Emma Porter started the Environment Group, which set up a cardboard and paper recycling program. To help the cafeteria workers to recycle cardboard, the group bought a trolley so they could transport the cardboard to the collection point. Paper that has been used on only one side is used to make notepads. Unley School also recycles as much plastic as possible.

Reuse

Now you might like to think creatively about how to reuse materials. As always, it is good to start with a survey. Find out how paper is reused. Many goods come in plastic containers—what happens to them once they are empty?

Your eco group could suggest some simple ideas for reusing items. Teachers and students can keep paper that has been used on one side for rough drafts. Plastic containers can be used to hold pens and pencils. Seedlings can be planted in old soda cans. When paper cannot be written on anymore, try using it for art projects, from papier mâché models to masks. The students at Lyrup Primary School, in South Australia, make their waste paper into bricks and sell them to local people for fuel! Here's how they do it: www.wow.sa.gov.au/uploads/pdfdocs/lyrupfinal.pdf.

Your art department should be able to reuse all kinds of materials. Here, papier mâché has been used to make a giant model of the planet Saturn.

Not every school can start a major project such as paper-brick making. So, how can individual students reuse materials? A good way is to use lunch boxes and refill water bottles instead of using plastic bags and bottles (see pages 38–39 for ideas).

Irish Eco-Schools reduce waste

- In 2008–2009, 13.2 tons of waste was diverted from **landfills** every school day by 3,200 Irish schools involved in the Eco-Schools program.
- About 3.7 million units of electricity, 44 million gallons (200 million liters) of drinking water, and around 110,000 gallons (500,000 liters) of fuel were saved in just one year.

Recycle

At the International School of Paris, France, they switched from using bleached white paper to using recycled paper throughout the school. They could recycle the paper again afterward. This kind of recycling is better for the environment than using a single-use product and throwing it straight into the recycling bin.

Buy a recycled product, such as paper.

Use it fully.

Once you can get no more use out of a product, then it is time to recycle it.

Recycle it.

Reuse the paper wisely.

Drinks in plastic bottles are refrigerated in stores, which uses a large amount of energy. Then, resources are used for recycling the bottle—if the user remembers to recycle it! See pages 40–41 for greener alternatives.

Successful school recycling

At Lothrop Science and Technology Magnet School, in North Omaha, Nebraska, the students take the lead. Older students run the recycling program, passing on their knowledge to younger children.

The project began during a science class. The students put on masks and thick gloves and emptied the garbage cans—a disgusting but instructive task! They separated the recyclable materials and realized many of the materials did not need to be thrown away.

The students devised a survey to see how the distance between recycling bins and garbage cans affects recycling rates. (People are more likely to recycle if there is a recycling bin nearby.) They discovered that if a recycling monitor stands by the recycling bins at lunchtime, this encourages others to use them.

Now, three students each week are on paper patrol. They have 15 minutes to collect recycling from classrooms around the school. In the cafeteria, students sort out the recyclable plastic and collect food waste for composting. They have succeeded in reducing cafeteria waste from 20 to just 2 bags a day. The school also collects batteries, electronics, and glasses for recycling.

This is an elementary school, so if they can do all of this, older students certainly can!

These Lothrop School students are putting their used containers into recycling bins.

Keep up the good work

Once you have a recycling program up and running, you will want to ensure it keeps going. What incentives can you use? At some schools, students who help to recycle can get special vouchers to use in the cafeteria, with bonus points if they help out with the recycling program after school. Students who have worked particularly hard for their school's recycling program have won prizes such as movie passes.

Boys at Downton Value School in Los Angeles are collecting food for the compost bin after lunch. The school also grows vegetables in a garden and in a greenhouse.

"Most classrooms and office areas have a box for cardboard [recycling]. Twice a term (more often in the office areas) and at the end of the year, we empty the boxes into the big white SITA dumpster."

Timothy Z, Portside Christian School, South Australia

Being green: Summing up

- Cut waste by reducing, reusing, and recycling.
- Focus on reducing use of paper and plastic products.
- Reuse paper for rough drafts or art projects.
- Take charge of recycling and encourage others.

Eco-Friendly Food

What fast and simple changes can you make so your food and drinks are more eco-friendly, cheaper, and better for you? First, assess yourself! Are you wasteful or waste-aware?

Check this list of **disposable** items to see how your packed lunch measures up:
- sandwich in a cardboard or plastic box
- salad in a plastic box
- chips, bars, or cookies in plastic packaging
- containers of yogurt
- carton or bottle of a drink
- plastic cutlery
- plastic bags.

If you have lots of disposable items in your lunch, consider the ideas below. Or if you're having pasta or rice for dinner, why not make a little extra to keep for lunch the next day?

1. Pick a carbohydrate (bread, pasta, rice).
2. Choose fresh vegetables in season or canned vegetables.
3. Add protein (prepared meat, canned fish, cheese, cooked beans).
4. Pack or chop fruit into natural yogurt (from a large carton).
5. Put your meal and yogurt into food containers.
6. Pour juice or water into a drink bottle (strong plastic or metal).

All the plastic food containers in this healthy packed lunch can be reused again and again.

Lunch tips

Try shopping on the weekend for packed-lunch items for the week. You can buy large sizes of goods, such as cartons of juice, which are cheaper and use less packaging than individual cartons. It will take only minutes to prepare your lunch each day. You will avoid long lines in the cafeteria, save money, and have more time for lunchtime activities.

Fresh fruit needs no preparation beyond washing—just place it in your lunch box.

Eco snacks

Of course, it can be hard to be organized enough to prepare food every day. At Ithaca Creek State Primary School, in Australia, workers at an on-site snack bar prepare sandwiches and salads with fresh ingredients—some of the produce comes from the school garden. They minimize food waste by only making meals or sandwiches when they are ordered. Any leftover food goes in the **wormery** along with fruit and vegetable peelings. The liquid from the wormery fertilizes the garden, and the whole cycle begins again!

Processed organic foods

Pre-packaged **organic** meals and snacks are convenient, but are they better for the environment?

- Pros: The ingredients are products of **organic farming**, which does not use chemical **fertilizers** that can harm wildlife.
- Cons: Processing food requires a large amount of energy. Once produced, processed foods are packaged, transported, and often chilled in a refrigerator—just like non-organic foods.

Think about your drink

There is nothing wrong with buying a soda or fruit drink every now and then when you're out. However, although some bottled drinks are healthy, many contain a large amount of sugar and additives, and they are not cheap. Also, packaging, transporting, and refrigerating the beverages come at a cost to the environment.

So, how can you cut down on costs and waste but stay hydrated and healthy? If you live in an economically developed country such as the United States, your home will have a fresh water supply—and it is probably cleaner and safer than bottled water. In some areas, the water is safe but does not taste good. You could talk to your family about buying a water filter to make tap water taste better.

Eco impact

A U.S. report in 2010 showed that:

- About 50 percent of bottled water is actually tap water in a plastic bottle.
- About 75 percent of the bottles are thrown away, not recycled.
- The plastic in some bottles leaches (leaks) a substance called phthalate into the water. Some studies have linked this chemical with hormonal problems in people.
- Bottled water goes through fewer safety tests than tap water.
- Bottled water costs 100 times as much as tap water! Bottled water typically costs just over $1 for 1 gallon (3.8 liters) and much more when you buy smaller bottles. Tap water costs about 1 cent per gallon.

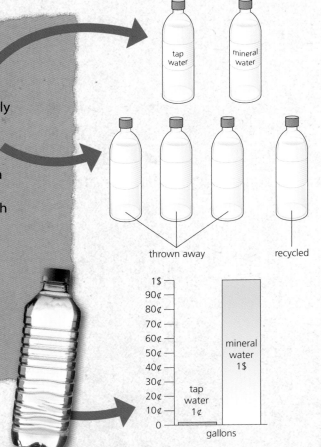

Be smart with smoothies

Do you like fruit smoothies or yogurt drinks? You could save cash and packaging by filling up a portable bottle from a large bottle at home, rather than buying small bottles. Even better, why not make your own smoothie with a blender? Fresh, soft fruit in season is tasty, or you can use canned fruit. Bananas are great blended with natural yogurt. It is easy and cheap to make your own smoothies.

Smoothie

You will need:

A few pieces of fruit, ideally two or three types, either fresh, canned, or a mixture

About 9 fl. oz. (250 ml) of fruit juice, either fresh or from concentrate

A few ice cubes or some cold water

Method:

1. Wash and chop any fresh fruit into small pieces.

2. Put all the ingredients in a blender and blend for about 30 seconds, until the mixture is smooth.

3. Add more juice or water if the smoothie is too thick.

4. If you have any left over, pour it into a popsicle mold and freeze to make a healthy, eco-friendly summer treat.

Growing food

There is a cheap and easy way to grow food at school—even if there are no flower beds! Cylinder gardening uses containers that can be placed almost anywhere. You don't need any gardening experience, and the preparation is simple. Why not give it a try?

Make a cylinder garden

You will need:

At least one 5-gallon (23-liter) bucket of the type used to transport food
  (you could ask a local restaurant to supply clean buckets)
Potting soil
Vegetable seeds
Fertilizer

Method:

1. Figure out where to place your cylinder garden. You can position it on top of soil or on a human-made surface, such as concrete. Try to find an area that will receive at least six to eight hours of sunlight and is close to a source of water.

2. Research vegetables that will grow during the season you are in. If you are gardening at school, look for varieties that you can harvest within a school quarter or semester—30 to 90 days. Search for compact varieties that can grow in a small space. The vegetables mentioned on page 47 are suitable for cylinder gardening, as are beans, carrots, parsley, peas, or tomatoes.

3. Cut off the bottom of the bucket and discard it. Then cut the rest of the bucket in half. You may need an adult to help you. Now you have two cylinders. (Note: If you are placing the bucket on concrete, it is better not to cut it, but ask an adult to drill drainage holes in the bottom.)

4. Put the cylinders in position.

5. Fill them with potting soil and mix in some fertilizer.

6. Plant your seeds, following the instructions on the package for spacing, and water gently.

7. Monitor the seedlings as they grow, keeping them moist with water and adding fertilizer regularly. **Thin out** the seedlings if they are crushed together.

Source: KidsGardening, www.kidsgardening.org

Food miles

Growing your own vegetables reduces **food miles**. The principle behind food miles is that the farther away your food is produced, the worse for the environment. However, keep in mind that beans that are produced locally using oil-based fertilizers and plowed by diesel tractors could be worse than beans grown by less energy-intensive methods in another country. Storing local food for a long time to be eaten out of season can also use up a lot of energy.

Being green: Summing up
- Make eco-friendly packed meals and snacks.
- Stay hydrated by drinking tap water and homemade smoothies.
- Grow your own food in a cylinder garden.

Nature and Biodiversity

Why would you bother encouraging nature and biodiversity at school? Well, you spend a lot of time at school, so it is worth making your school grounds more attractive. Most students find nature and outdoor education programs engaging and enjoyable. Also, a school nature project can be large enough to make a difference to local wildlife.

Small creatures such as bees, beetles, spiders, and snails form an essential part of the food chain. Solitary bees are essential for pollinating flowers; spiders eat insect pests; and snails provide food for birds and other small animals. Taking care of these small creatures is important, but few modern gardens have natural areas where they can take shelter. So, how about making a bug hotel in the fall to keep the insects and snails snug during winter?

Make a bug hotel

You will need:

10 square feet (1 square meter) of plastic mesh or chicken wire
Plastic-covered garden wire, twine, or garden string
Several dead plant stems or twigs
Pile of fallen leaves
Flat piece of wood or plastic (big enough to cover the top end
  of the mesh when it has been made into a tube)
Two or three large rocks
A few tent pegs

Did you know?
- We need insects to produce honey, chocolate, coffee, and silk.
- Insects are a vital food source for birds and animals.
- About 90 percent of wildflowers could be threatened with extinction (being wiped out) if there were no insects to pollinate them.

Method:

1. Decide where to put your bug hotel. A quiet corner in the shade is best.

2. Curl the plastic mesh or chicken wire into a tube. Tie it in place using four twists of garden wire.

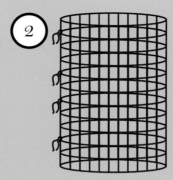

3. Poke some dead plant stems or twigs through the sides of the cylinder at the bottom. They should overlap to form a mesh, which will stop the leaves from falling out of the bottom if you move the bug hotel. They will also stop the leaves from touching the ground and becoming damp.

4. Now loosely fill the cylinder with dead leaves.

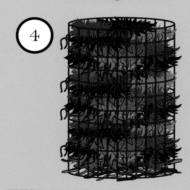

5. Use the piece of wood to make a lid. Place rocks on top to keep it secure.

6. If your bug hotel is in a windy position, you can pin the cylinder to the ground using tent pegs.

Source: Buglife, www.buglife.org.uk

Make the most of your space

This raised bed is perfect for growing a variety of vegetables in addition to wildflowers to attract wildlife. It is handy if you have a concrete patio or a small garden.

Build a no-dig raised garden bed

You will need:

Four planks of recycled wood to make a rectangle for the bed. Any length from 3 ft. (1 m) upward is fine. The depth should be at least 6 in. (15 cm).
4 brackets and galvanized screws to secure them
Several old cardboard boxes, more than enough to cover the base of the bed
Several old newspapers
A wheelbarrow or large tub for wetting the newspaper
Alfalfa hay
Manure
Straw
Some potting compost

Method:

1. Decide where to place the bed—either on bare earth or grass. Lay out the planks of wood.

2. Place brackets over the corners where the planks meet and screw them in. You may need an adult to help.

3. Lay the cardboard on the base of the bed, making sure it overlaps.

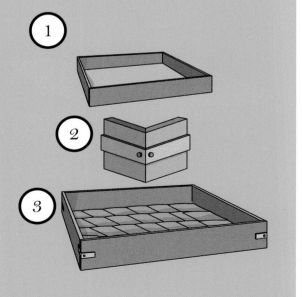

4. Put the newspaper in a wheelbarrow or large plastic tub and pour some water over it.

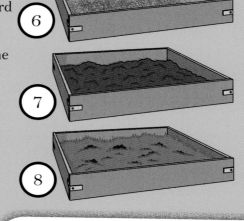

5. Spread the wet newspaper over the cardboard, making sure the layers overlap by one-third of their size. Make sure the entire surface is covered, to cut out the light. The cardboard and paper will rot down into the soil.

6. Add a layer of alfalfa hay. This will feed the soil as it breaks down.

7. Add a thin layer of manure.

8. Finally, add a layer of straw. This adds **nutrients** and acts as a mulch, keeping plants warm in winter and holding in moisture in summer.

9. Make small holes in the top layer of straw to make space for your plants. Add a handful of potting compost in each hole before putting in the plants.

Source: No Dig Vegetable Garden, www.no-dig-vegetablegarden.com

Easy-to-grow veggies

You can plant these vegetables directly in your raised bed:

- Lettuce: Try "cut and come again" varieties. Once the lettuces are big, just cut off what you need and leave them to continue growing.
- Radishes: These don't need much care. You may need to thin them out if the seedlings sprout too close together.
- Spinach: These can be easy to grow. You can often pick off leaves and the plant will keep growing.
- Chard: This is similar to spinach and has colorful red stems.
- Onions: It is simplest to plant onion sets, which are tiny onions.
- Potatoes: They are easy to grow, but they need plenty of water.

Bringing It Together: Kent Meridian High School

Kent Meridian High School in Kent, Washington, is a Bronze level Eco-School and part of the Cool School Challenge, an environmental program.

For the Cool School Challenge, environmental science teacher Dianne Thompson and her students carried out an energy review. Student Asha Salim reports: "The students and Mrs. Thompson's environmental science class go into the other classes and have a one-on-one discussion with the teachers about how much energy they're using and what they can do to reduce it." The students then offer tips to the teachers on how to cut down their energy use. In a few months, they go back and see how much energy those teachers have saved.

The students also tackle water waste. First, they undertake a water assessment, going around the school looking for leaking faucets. They produce a report for the custodian and then the principal. The last time they did this, they discovered six leaking faucets that needed repairing.

This urban garden has been created by cleverly stacking wooden beds to make the best use of the available space and light.

Strawberries make a great addition to an edible garden.

Recycling is an essential element of the program. Edros Palisoc describes recycling at Kent Meridian, saying: "We recycle in the whole school … At lunch we have students who monitor the kids who have lunch to tell them which items are recyclable."

The school has a garden that attracts all kinds of wildlife, including songbirds, hummingbirds, and butterflies. There is a pond that contains fish. There is also an edible garden. As Deven Moss explains: "The edible garden is … being used for the cooking class. They can use the food there instead of having to find produce elsewhere to use." No **pesticides** are used to grow the crops.

This case study shows how many people in the school working together have succeeded in reducing energy use and water waste, increasing recycling, and encouraging wildlife. They are eco stars!

Being green: Summing up

- Take part in school nature programs.
- Make a bug hotel to attract insects.
- Build a raised bed to grow vegetables and wildflowers.
- Many schools around the world have gone green. Maybe your school can, too!

Quiz

Are you an eco star or an energy guzzler? Take this quiz to find out! See page 55 for the results.

1. **When you're at home during cold weather, do you . . .**
   a) crank up the heating so it is as hot as a sauna?
   b) keep the heating on all the time to keep the house warm?
   c) put the heating on for a few hours a day and wear a cozy sweater or snuggle up with a warm blanket if you are cold?

2. **In your house, do you switch off lights and gadgets as soon as you have finished using them?**
   a) No, I leave them on in case someone else wants to use them.
   b) I turn off the lights but leave gadgets on standby, so it takes less effort to turn them on again later.
   c) Yes, I turn everything off—it is a waste of energy otherwise.

3. **Do you use the shower or bath?**
   a) There's nothing like a long, hot soak in a deep bath!
   b) I use the shower, but I like a long, luxurious one.
   c) I take a quick, refreshing shower to save time and energy.

4. **How do you use water when you brush your teeth?**
   a) I run the faucet while I'm brushing—it saves effort!
   b) I run the faucet to wash my toothbrush and rinse my mouth.
   c) I fill a cup with water to rinse my mouth and the toothbrush.

5. **Are you an eco shopper?**
   a) More so a shopaholic! I have no willpower to resist the latest gadgets and accessories.
   b) I try to buy just the items I really need.
   c) I love rummaging in thrift stores and rarely buy new goods.

6. **How much do you recycle?**
   a) I don't bother. It's not going to change the world, is it?
   b) I recycle paper, cardboard, cans, and bottles.
   c) Almost everything—I'm a total expert. I even know where to take old DVDs and batteries for recycling.

7. **Do you have green fingers?**
   a) What, hang around in a muddy garden in the wind and rain? You've got to be joking.
   b) I've tried growing some plants at home, but they usually die.
   c) Yes! I know how to care for plants and can raise easy-to-grow vegetables and herbs.

8. **If you buy food or snacks when you're out, what do you do with the packaging?**
   a) I throw it in the garbage if there's one right there, otherwise on the ground.
   b) I look for a garbage can or a recycling bin.
   c) I keep the packaging to wash and recycle once I get home.

9. **How do you mostly travel around?**
   a) I like being driven around. I hate getting cold and wet when the weather's bad.
   b) I sometimes get a lift in the car, but I use the bus, walk, or cycle to some places.
   c) I rarely go anywhere by car. I walk, cycle, or use public transportation.

10. **If you need to take a packed meal . . .**
   a) I buy everything pre-packaged to save time.
   b) I make a sandwich or some pasta and take a carton of juice and a yogurt or snack bar for convenience.
   c) I make a sandwich or take some tasty cooked food from the refrigerator and some fresh fruit.

Glossary

biodiversity variety of plants and animals in a particular habitat or the world

climate change rising temperatures worldwide, caused by the increase of greenhouse gases in the atmosphere that trap the Sun's heat

compact fluorescent lightbulb energy-saving lightbulb. It is more efficient than an incandescent lightbulb and lasts much longer.

conservation protecting wild habitats and their plants and animals

disposable made to be thrown away after being used once

draft proofing blocking up unwanted gaps that let in cold air, in order to save energy

energy-efficient using as little energy as possible for a task

fertilizer product added to soil or water to provide extra nutrients to help plants grow

flow meter bag bag with markings to measure the volume of water flowing in from a faucet or shower

flow rate amount of liquid that flows in a given time—for example, 2.5 gallons per minute

flow restrictor gadget designed to limit the amount of liquid that flows out of a faucet or shower

food miles distance that foods travel from the point of origin to your table

fossil fuel energy source, such as coal, gas, and oil, that was formed over millions of years from the remains of animals or plants

incandescent lightbulb type of lightbulb commonly used in homes. It is not energy-efficient and is gradually being phased out.

kilowatt hour measurement of electricity use over an hour. A kilowatt hour is when you use 1,000 watts of energy in an hour—for example, using a 1,000-watt oven for one hour.

landfill area of land where large amounts of waste material are buried under the earth

lumens measurement of the amount of visible light a bulb gives out

mulch organic matter, such as leaves, straw, or bark chippings, that is placed around the base of plants to improve the quality of the soil

nectar-rich rich in nectar, a sweet liquid produced by flowers and collected by bees for making honey

nongovernmental organization nonprofit organization that is not part of the government and works to help people

nutrient chemical that nourishes living things

organic produced without using human-made chemicals

organic farming method of farming that minimizes the use of harmful chemical fertilizers and pesticides. Organic farming is also known as all-natural farming.

pesticide chemical used to kill insects or other organisms that are harmful to crops

pollinate put pollen into a plant so that it produces seeds

prevailing wind wind from the direction that is most common in a particular place or season

public liability insurance insurance to cover a group or event in case money has to be paid out to members of the public because of an injury or damage to property

risk assessment careful examination of what could cause harm to people

sustainable way of doing something that does not use up too many natural resources or pollute the environment

thermal imaging measuring the surface temperature—for example, of a house—so that people can figure out where heat is being lost

thin out remove weaker seedlings to allow space for the stronger ones to grow well

watt unit of power that measures the rate of using electricity

wind turbine huge fan that turns the moving energy of the wind into useful energy

wormery compost bin containing worms that are particularly effective at breaking down food waste, including cooked food

Find Out More

Further reading

Gay, Kathlyn. *Living Green: The Ultimate Teen Guide*. Lanham, Md.: Scarecrow, 2012.

Johnson, J. Angelique. *The Eco-Student's Guide to Being Green at School*. Mankato, Minn.: Picture Window, 2011.

Petronis, Lexi, Karen Macklin, and Jill Buck. *47 Things You Can Do for the Environment*. Boston: Houghton Mifflin Harcourt, 2012.

Savedge, Jenn. *The Green Teen: The Eco-Friendly Teen's Guide to Saving the Planet*. Gabriola Island, B.C.: New Society, 2009.

Sivertsen, Linda, and Tosh Sivertsen. *Generation Green: The Ultimate Teen Guide to Living an Eco-Friendly Life*. New York: Simon Pulse, 2008.

Smith, Sharon J. *The Young Activist's Guide to Building a Green Movement and Changing the World*. Berkeley: Ten Speed, 2011.

Web sites

www.eco-schools.org
This is the web site for the international Eco-Schools campaign.

www.epa.gov/epahome/community.htm#conditions
The Environmental Protection Agency (EPA) has lots of information about protecting the environment in your community.

www.epa.gov/students
This is the part of the EPA site created specifically for students.

globalstewards.org
This web site has a list of ways to reduce, reuse, and recycle.

www.greenecocommunities.com
This is a resource for eco-friendly communities and homes.

www.nwf.org/Global-Warming/School-Solutions/Eco-Schools-USA.aspx
This offers information about the Eco-Schools movement in the United States.

www.thedailygreen.com/going-green/6334
This web site offers tips for teens about going green in daily life.

DVDs

The Age of Stupid, director Franny Armstrong (New Video, 2010)

Food, Inc, director Robert Kenner (Magnolia, 2009)

An Inconvenient Truth, director Davis Guggenheim (Paramount, 2006)

More topics to research

Once you have read this book, you might like to research Eco-Schools in your area—perhaps you could link up with them and share ideas? It could be exciting to make contact with a school in another country, too. You may also want to find out what your local government is doing to protect the environment. Perhaps your eco group could come up with suggestions for how to promote eco policies to young people.

Answers to box question (page 28):
You would need to buy about 21 bulbs that last 850 hours to get 18,000 hours of service (21 x 850 = 17,850 hours). Those 21 bulbs will cost you $117.60. So, the $62 bulb is a better buy.

Answers to quiz (pages 50–51):
Mostly As:
Sounds like you're an energy guzzler, but at least you're aware of it. Pick just a couple of ideas from this book and start being a little more eco-friendly.

Mostly Bs:
You're clearly making an effort. Look for a few ideas in this book to do more.

Mostly Cs:
You're an eco star! Keep up the good work and spread the message to others.

Index